D0820625

The Story of Science

Earth's Place
in Space

by Roy A. Gallant

BENCHMARK BOOKS

MARSHALL CAVENDISH
NEW YORK

Series Editor: Roy A. Gallant

Series Consultants:

LIFE SCIENCES
Dr. Edward J. Kormondy
Chancellor and Professor of Biology (retired)
University of Hawaii—Hilo/West Oahu

PHYSICAL SCIENCES
Dr. Jerry LaSala, Chairman
Department of Physics
University of Southern Maine

Benchmark Books
Marshall Cavendish Corporation
99 White Plains Road
Tarrytown, NY 10591-9001

Library of Congress Cataloging-in-Publication Data
Gallant, Roy A.
        Earth's place in space / by Roy A. Gallant.
        p. cm. — (The story of science series)
Includes bibliographical references and index.
Summary: Relates the history of the struggle to understand earth's place in the universe, from earliest myth-making to today's discoveries via the Hubble telescope.
ISBN 0-7614-0963-7
        1. Earth—Juvenile literature. 2. Cosmology—Juvenile literature. [1. Earth. 2. Cosmology. 3. Universe.] I. Title. II. Series: Gallant, Roy A. The story of science series.
QB631.4.G355   1999   525—dc21   98-28043   CIP   AC

Photo research by Jeannine L. Dickey and Linda Sykes Photo Research, Hilton Head, SC.
Diagrams on pp. 18, 21, 27, 30, 33, 42, 43, 57, 67, 69 by Jeannine L. Dickey
COVER: NASA Art Collecction
Title page NASA; 6 Corbis-Bettmann; 8 Weik, Edmund, Bilderatlas der Steinenwelt, 1892; 11 Palazzo Farnese, Caprarola/Scala/Art Resource; 13 Bib. Nat./Superstock; 15 www.arttoday.com; 19 Association of Universities for Research in Astronomy, Inc. (AURA), all rights reserved; 20 Vic Winter, ICSTARS Astronomy; 22 Stock Montage; 22 The Granger Collection, New York; 26 Stock Montage; 26 The Granger Collection, New York; 28 Newberry Library, Chicago/Superstock; 29 Royal Academy of Arts, London/Superstock; 31 Corbis-Bettmann; 36 Superstock; 38 The Granger Collection, New York; 41 The Granger Collection, New York; 44 (inset) The Granger Collection, New York; 44 Ronan Picture Library; 48 NASA; 49 (left) Association of Universities for Research in Astronomy, Inc. (AURA), all rights reserved; 49 (right) Todd Borogon/NOAO; 52 NASA; 52 NASA; 52 NASA; 53 NASA; 54 Corbis-Bettmann; 57 Hale Observatories; 60 South African Astronomical Observatory, Cape Town, South Africa; 60 (inset) Association of Universities for Research in Astronomy, Inc.(AURA), all rights reserved; 62 NASA; 63 NASA

Printed in Hong Kong
6 5 4 3 2 1

Cover photo: Servicing the Hubble Space Telescope, the instrument that has given us the most beautiful, awe-inspiring, and informative views of the Universe. This painting by John Solie shows astronaut Kathy Thornton releasing one of Hubble's defective solar panels into space. A second astronaut is seen at work in space shuttle *Endeavour*'s cargo bay.

In memory of the late historian of science
Colin A. Ronan

Contents

One

Dragons, Sun Gods, and Myths

The Myth Makers

We will never know if people of long ago regarded the sky more in wonder or more in fear. Certainly it was a bit of each. We know that comets were looked on as messengers of doom, or as the souls of heroes on their way to heaven. The unusual sky events were the ones that commanded attention—meteor showers, eclipses of the Sun and the Moon, and those flaming fireballs called bolides. Such sky events must have left some people scratching their heads in wonder and sent others crawling under the bed. Not understanding the natural causes of such cosmic happenings, people invented supernatural causes. They filled the sky with gods, demons, and spirits both evil and friendly.

Comets were among the spectacular sky events that struck terror into the hearts of people in ages past. Some believed that a comet was the soul of a departed ruler on its way to heaven. This photograph of comet Hale-Bopp, taken by Jim White March 26, 1997 from Trout Lake, Washington, shows a double tail. The blue tail is the ion tail made up of charged gas particles. The white tail is the dust tail made up of cast-off matter from the comet's nucleus.

The famous Leonid meteor storm of 1833 scared millions of people out of their wits on the night of November 12-13. The sky seemed ablaze with thousands of meteors and exploding bolides that left twisted tails. Some of the trains of glowing dust reportedly lasted up to twenty minutes. Many people thought the Day of Judgment had finally arrived and that the world was about to end.

They also imagined the stars as forming those figures we recognize today as the *constellations*. The constellations are ageless. The earliest known list of them was left by the Greek poet Aratus of Soli, who lived around 270 B.C. He listed forty-four constellations, which he claimed to have gotten from the works of the astronomer Eudoxus, who lived about a century earlier. Over the years, more constellations were added to the list, until today the official number is eighty-eight. Each constellation had a story to tell, a myth describing the heroic deeds of a hunter or the tragic tale of a vain and boastful queen. The sky became a vast storybook and a battlefield, where gods and demons fought in deadly combat and controlled the lives of mortals. The purpose of that cosmic storybook was to help people understand Earth's place in the Universe. And that search continues to this day.

An Earth-Centered Universe

Around 2000 B.C. people known as the Babylonians lived in what is now Iraq. Their spiritual leaders were astronomer-priests who observed the sky and recorded everything. Based on what they saw, these astronomer-priests developed several ideas about Earth and its place in the world. Some of their ideas were just like those that you or I would almost surely form on seeing the night sky for the first time and being asked to explain what we see.

One such idea was that Earth was the center of the world. Another was that Earth did not move. And still another was that the stars, Sun, and all other sky objects revolve, or circle, about Earth. After all, that is what our senses tell us, and seeing is all too often believing. Like the Sun by day, the stars by night seemed to rise in the east, move across the great sky dome, and set in the west. Like soldiers on parade, the stars were seen to move as a group, never seeming to change position in relation to each other. So the stars were called *fixed stars*.

Some "stars," however, looked bigger than the others. Also, they were not fixed but could be seen to wander among the field of less bright stars. These objects were called *wandering stars*. Two such objects were the planets Mercury and Venus. They stayed fairly close to the Sun and always moved right along with it. They were seen only briefly before sunrise or for a short time after sunset, at which time they disappeared for a while into the "underworld."

The Moon was a special object of mystery. It was seen to change its shape from one night to the next, as it glided eastward among the stars and went through a cycle of phases. One complete cycle, from one full moon to the next full moon, took about twenty-nine-and-a-half days as it was seen to move eastward among the background stars. The Sun seemed never to change, except for its daily motion from east to west across the sky by day, and its slow west-to-east creep across the sky throughout the year. Also, the noon-day Sun always climbed higher in the sky in summer than in winter. The height of the great sky dome was unknown to those ancient astronomers. Surely it was higher than the mountains, but how much higher no one could say.

There were three other wanderers, and their motions seemed especially puzzling. Unlike Mercury and Venus, they sometimes

That the sky was a vast story book where gods and demons fought in deadly combat and controlled the lives of mortals is evidenced in this fresco showing part of the Zodiac and painted in the mid-1500s. The artist was Taddeo Zucarri. The painting is part of a series about the Zodiac in the Palazzo Farnese in Caprarola, Italy.

10

were visible for several hours in the night sky, long after sunset or long before sunrise. They were Mars, Jupiter, and Saturn. Along with Mercury and Venus, today we call them *planets*. The word comes from the Greek *planasthai*, meaning "to wander." The remaining planets, Uranus, Neptune, and Pluto, were too faint to be seen without a telescope. They were to remain invisible for more than three thousand years after the Babylonians lived. The telescope was not to be invented until the early 1600s.

The especially puzzling motion of Mars, Jupiter, and Saturn

was not understood for many centuries. All three planets generally wandered eastward among the background stars, in the opposite direction of the stars' motion as a group. Even more puzzling was that from time to time each planet was seen to slow down, come to a stop, then back up, swinging around in a loop before resuming its eastward motion again. As our story of Earth's place in space unfolds, we will return to this looping motion and see how it was eventually explained.

Another puzzling feature of the night sky was that broad hazy band of light seen to stretch across the sky on any clear night. Today we call it the *Milky Way*. An understanding of its nature also had to wait many centuries. The ancient Greeks accounted for it in their mythology by saying it was milk spilled by the infant Hercules when he was being nursed by the goddess Juno.

The old Babylonian astronomer-priests came to know the eastward paths their five known planets traced as they moved among the stars. Year after year those planets were seen to cross through the same constellations. It was also the same path the Sun and the Moon followed. All passed through twelve constellations that formed that circular celestial highway that we know as the *zodiac*. The "center line" along that highway was the Sun's path and is called the *ecliptic*.

All seven wanderers—including the Sun and the Moon—seemed to revolve around Earth. Who could deny this? It was what anyone could see by watching the sky day and night. Further, Earth stood motionless at the very center of all that was. Surely Earth must be the very center of creation itself. Although the astronomer-priests kept accurate records of the motions of heavenly objects, they never developed scientific models based on those records, models that would show how the Universe is put together and how its many parts move.

Stargazers of old observed that the planets, the Sun, and the Moon all appeared to trace a path across the sky that took them through twelve constellations that came to be known as the Zodiac. Each constellation took up a space of 30 degrees across the sky, for a total to 360 degrees or one complete trip around the sky. Starting with the constellation Aries the Ram, at the ten o'clock position, the other eleven constellations surrounding the central Sun were Pisces the Fishes, Aquarius the Water Bearer, Capricorn the Goat, Sagittarius the Archer, Scorpio the Scorpion, Libra the Balance, Virgo the Virgin, Leo the Lion, Cancer the Crab, Gemini the Twins, and Taurus the Bull.

Two

From Myth to Measurement

The day was bound to come when a new breed of sky watchers came along—people who regarded the old myths as nothing more than fairy tales in the sky. For instance, they could no longer accept as fact that each morning a sacred boat or golden chariot carried the Sun god up over the eastern horizon and across the sky. Or that at night the sacred boat descended below the western horizon and continued its journey through the "underworld." Or that a new day dawned when the boat emerged from the underworld and once again rose in the east.

In place of the old myths, the new sky watchers did what the astronomer-priests of ancient times had failed to do. They used the numerous records of the changing positions of the Sun, the Moon, and planets to design physical models that showed how the Universe worked.

In Greek Mythology, Helios was the Sun god. Each morning he appeared out of the east and crossed the sky in a golden chariot. By day's end, his journey finished, he disappeared over the western horizon.

The Spheres of Eudoxus

In the Western world the search for natural causes of events in the sky began sometime around 600 B.C. One of the new breed of sky watchers was the Greek astronomer Eudoxus. He is best known for trying to explain the apparent motions of the stars, the Sun, the Moon, and planets. He imagined that the fixed stars were all the same distance from Earth and were attached to a huge invisible glass sphere. His great star sphere slowly turned, carrying the fixed stars around and so accounting for their rising in the east and setting in the west. All the while, Earth sat motionless at the center. The Sun was attached to another sphere closer to Earth. As that sphere turned it carried the Sun around Earth. The Moon also had a sphere that carried it

around Earth. The nesting spheres model of Eudoxus worked well enough for the apparent motion of the stars, the Sun, and the Moon. But what about the more difficult looping movements of the planets?

To account for their back-and-forth motions, he had to add still more nesting spheres. Eventually his model had so many spheres within spheres that it became hopelessly complex. Later, Aristotle also imagined such a model of nesting spheres, but his ended up with so many spheres—fifty-six—that he had to give it up. Further, neither model could account for eclipses, for instance. The important thing, however, was that these Greek thinkers were trying to reason out a problem by using mathematics and geometry rather than continuing to blindly accept the old myths.

A Shape and Size for Earth

One of the greatest of the ancient Greek thinkers was Aristotle, who was born in 384 B.C. Aristotle rejected the popular belief that Earth was flat. The Greek mathematician Pythagoras had come to the same conclusion about two hundred years earlier. You can see for yourself that Earth is not flat, Aristotle explained. Just watch a ship sail over the horizon. First the hull slowly lowers from sight, then the mast. It is clear that the ship is not sinking, for a few days later it safely returns to port. Does this not prove that the oceans are curved and not flat, even though they appear flat? he asked. Also, during an eclipse of the Moon, he said, Earth's curved shadow cast on the Moon shows that Earth is a sphere, not flat. As convincing as his arguments seemed, not everyone believed him. They could not understand why, if Earth were a sphere, people on the underside did not fall off, or how they managed to walk "upside down." Discovery of the law of *gravitation*, which would explain these things, was still two thousand years in the future.

At the time we are talking about, no one knew Earth's size. Although Aristotle tried to measure the distance around Earth, he came up with a figure much too small. And nothing was known about the size of or distance to the Sun, the Moon, or stars.

Around 230 B.C. the Greek geographer and mathematician Eratosthenes lived in Alexandria, Egypt, where he was head of the world's then greatest library. He was the first to measure Earth's size accurately. He reasoned that since Earth's surface was curved, the noon Sun must strike two cities far apart at different angles. By measuring those angles, and then measuring how far apart the cities were, he was able to estimate Earth's circumference. His measurement was only 125 miles (200 kilometers) in error. Today we know that Earth's circumference is 24,730 miles (39,800 kilometers). The discovery that Earth was so large amazed scholars of the time.

Distances to the Sun and the Moon

While Eratosthenes was carrying out his work in Alexandria, one of the most remarkable astronomers of ancient times was at work on the Greek island of Samos. His name was Aristarchus, and he was intent on measuring the distances and sizes of the Moon and the Sun. He tried to measure the angle between the Sun and the Moon when the Moon was half full. Although the idea was sound, the measurement was impossible to make accurately enough to calculate the Sun's actual distance from Earth. He said the Sun was twenty times more distant than the Moon, far short of the Sun's actual distance. Today we know that the Sun is nearly four hundred times the Moon's distance. Even though Aristarchus's measurement was way off, it suggested that the

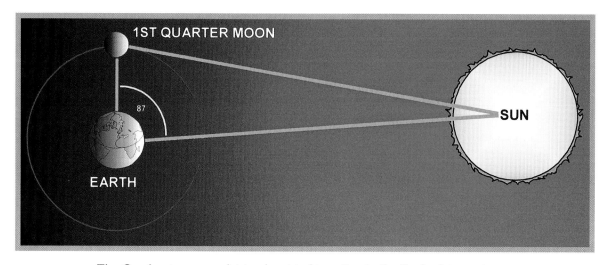

The Greek astronomer Aristarchus tried to estimate the Sun's distance by saying how many times farther away it is than the Moon's distance. The angle at (A) would have to be less than 90 degrees when the Moon was at first quarter. Aristarchus's measurement showed 87 degrees. Because the angles were extremely difficult to measure accurately, Aristarchus's distance for the Sun was far too short—only 20 times more distant than the Moon. Aristarchus lived from about 310 B.C. to about 230 B.C.

Sun was farther away than anyone had imagined. And that meant that it must be very large, considering its apparent size.

The remarkable thing about Aristarchus was not his distance measurements, but his ideas about the heavens. He said that the Sun—not Earth—was at the center of the Universe. He further thought that all the planets circled the Sun, including Earth. He further said that the sphere of stars did not move, but that it was Earth's *rotation*, or spinning around like a top, that made the star sphere appear to move. Although Aristarchus had several reasons to support his plan of the heavens, he was not able to show any evidence for it. Without that convincing evidence, there was little reason to abandon the old idea. The truth of his ideas would have to wait nearly two thousand years.

Meanwhile, Aristarchus's attempts to measure the Sun's distance sparked interest in others to try their hand. One was the greatest astronomer of ancient times, Hipparchus. His method of measuring the Sun's distance from Earth was to time the Moon's passage through Earth's shadow during a lunar eclipse. Even though the idea was sound, the measurement is too difficult to make accurately. His distance to the Sun came out to only 9 million miles (15 million kilometers). Although ten times too short, it was better than Aristarchus's distance and greatly increased the height of the great sky dome.

Around 150 B.C. Hipparchus measured the Moon's distance and size quite accurately, to within 1 percent. But his most important work came from his skills as an expert observer of the night sky. Two examples will show why. First, he drew a chart of the heavens by showing his carefully measured positions of 850 stars. He also included their *apparent brightness* compared with

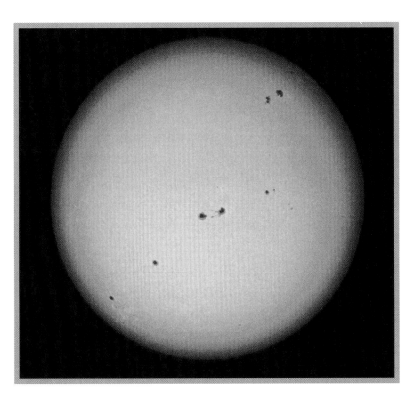

Once we know the Sun's distance, we can figure out its size. We can measure the Sun's apparent diameter, or how wide across the Sun looks from its great distance from us. Then by doing some fancy arithmetic, we can work out its actual diameter. That distance across the Sun's disk turns out to be 864,000 miles (1,390,000 kilometers). That is broad enough to allow 110 Earths to be strung across the Sun's face. The Sun is large enough to hold a million Earths inside. The dark spots in this photograph are sunspot magnetic storms.

Hipparchus worked out the Moon's distance and size quite accurately by measuring the size of Earth's shadow cast on the Moon during a lunar eclipse. Today we know the Moon's average distance from us to be 238,860 miles (384,400 kilometers). Its diameter is 2,160 miles (3,467 kilometers).

one another, termed apparent visual *magnitude*. Hipparchus's magnitude scale had six classes of brightness and is used to this day by astronomers. His chart was the first full list of visible stars ever to be made.

As he worked on his chart, Hipparchus compared his star positions with the positions of certain bright stars plotted earlier by two other astronomers. He was surprised to find that his position for the bright star Spica did not agree with that star's position recorded fifty years earlier on the other chart. It turned out that both positions, although different, were correct. It took him some time to figure out why. Spica had not moved, but Earth had. The reason for the motion, called *precession*, was not to be understood until many centuries later. The Sun's and the Moon's gravitational tug on Earth are such that they twist our planet this way and that. The result is that Earth wobbles on its axis like a spinning top slowing down. One complete wobble-circle takes about 25,800 years. So it was precession that was behind the Spica mystery.

From about 600 B.C. until the time Hipparchus died, around 120 B.C., the myths of old that had tried to explain everything that could be seen in the sky gradually lost their power. They were replaced by a new way of thinking about the world—called science. And the first science was *astronomy*, the study of the heavens and all they contain, including the distances, motions, and composition of the stars, planets, cosmic dust, and all other celestial bodies.

Because Earth wobbles on its axis, there is a gradual shift in the pattern and apparent motions of sky objects. For instance, the North Star is the star Polaris today, but in about 7,000 years the bright star Deneb in the constellation Cygnus the Swan will have its turn to be the North Star.

21

Three

Enter the Giants

Ptolemy and Epicycles

No history of astronomy book would be complete without the name Claudius Ptolemaeus, better known as Ptolemy. He lived around A.D. 130 and was the last of that long line of ancient Greek scholars. His views were published in his most important book, given the Arabic title *Almagest*, meaning the greatest. And his views set the climate of astronomical thinking for the next 1,500 years. Unfortunately, many of his views were wrong.

Ptolemy rejected Aristarchus's idea of a Sun-centered Universe. Instead he supported the old but incorrect Earth-centered system championed by Aristotle. He also rejected the idea that

The last great astronomer of ancient times, Ptolemy, being guided by the Muse of Astronomy as he observes the Moon. Ptolemy taught, incorrectly, that Earth stood at the center of the Universe. In his world system, the Sun revolved about a motionless Earth. Next came the Moon, Mercury, Venus, Mars, Jupiter, and Saturn. Beyond Saturn, there were no other planets, only the fixed stars as represented by the constellations of the Zodiac. Ptolemy lived around A.D. 150.

Earth spins around and so just makes it look as if the Sun and stars parade across the sky, where actually they don't. If Earth turned, he said, birds would be whipped off their perches. Ptolemy is best remembered for his attempt to explain the looping motions of the planets.

The idea he offered actually goes back to an astronomer named Apollonius, who had worked with Eratosthenes at the library in Alexandria. Ptolemy put some finishing touches on Apollonius's complex system of circles, called *epicycles*, which he said the planets traced as they circle Earth. Although incorrect, his model did account for the planets' looped paths, but only over periods of a few years.

The Arabs as Preservers

From the time of Ptolemy's death up to about the 1500s, there were almost no new ideas in astronomy. Christian and Islamic religious leaders preached that the only worthwhile knowledge was knowledge of God. If the books of earlier times did not praise God's work, then the books must be burned. So one after another, the great libraries and centers of learning were burned to the ground, including the greatest one of all, in Alexandria.

However, in the early 800s the enlightened Arab ruler, Caliph Hārūn-al-Rashīd, did not approve of the burning and destruction. He started a library of his own in Baghdad, called the House of Wisdom. Scholars came to him and brought priceless copies of old Greek texts. The texts were translated into Arabic and were preserved. Among them was Ptolemy's great book.

The Arabs made many fine instruments to measure star and planet positions. It was they who discovered that Ptolemy's system of epicycles did not work over long periods to accurately predict the planets' week-by-week position changes. To this day stars with Arabic names—such as Algol, Zubenelgenubi, Betelgeuse—remind us of the important role the Arabs played in astronomy.

Copernicus Starts a Revolution

By the 1500s a new spirit of learning began to spread over Europe. Scholars began reading books written by the old Greek masters and preserved by the Arabs. One such person was the Polish astronomer Nicolaus Copernicus. Like Aristarchus, Copernicus felt that a planetary system with the Sun at the center and with Earth and the other planets circling the Sun made more sense than Ptolemy's Earth-centered system. Copernicus also agreed that the apparent motions of the Sun and stars across the sky were caused by Earth rotating on its axis. It took Copernicus thirty years to work out the mathematical details of a new Solar System. When finished, his work became the greatest scientific achievement since Greek times. So powerful and so convincing were his ideas that they became known as the Copernican revolution.

Copernicus's great book was published in 1543 with the title *On the Revolutions of the Heavenly Spheres*. He feared that it would upset some scholars, and especially Roman Catholic Church leaders. The official view of the church was that Earth stood still, and that Earth—not the Sun—was the center of the Universe. When his book was published Copernicus had been seriously ill, and within hours after first seeing a printed copy, he died. He died never realizing two important things that his Solar System model revealed. First, epicycles were no longer needed to explain the planets' looped paths, but he felt they were needed to explain the planets' different speeds across the sky. Those loops were not real motions at all, only an optical illusion, or visual trick. The illusion is caused by our observing the other

The Polish astronomer Nicolaus Copernicus was the first to make a strong case for the Sun being at the center of the Solar System, with Earth and the other planets revolving about the Sun. Copernicus also reasoned that Earth turns on its axis. That motion, which produced day and night, also made the stars appear to parade across the sky from east to west. Copernicus lived from 1473 to 1543.

planets from a planet that is itself moving around the Sun. And second, he continued to believe that the stars were stuck to a great sphere that marked the outer limit of the Universe. It is unlikely that Copernicus ever realized that his great work was to lead astronomers toward our modern view of our Solar System home, and toward an understanding of Earth's place in space.

Tycho Paves the Way

Many scholars found Copernicus's work convincing. Others did not. One who did not was Tycho Brahe, a young Danish astronomer with a fiery temper. When a student, he once argued with another student over a mathematical problem, and the argument ended in a duel. Tycho lost. He also lost part of his nose. For the rest of his life he wore a false nose made of gold and silver.

Copernicus's model of a Sun-centered Solar System needed lots of evidence. That evidence would have to come from many detailed observations of the planets' changing positions in the sky. Tycho could not accept Copernicus's ideas for three reasons.

Ancient stargazers couldn't understand why Mars, Jupiter, and Saturn every now and then seemed to make a loop as they moved across the sky from west to east. Copernicus explained the optical illusion. As faster-moving Earth catches up with and then passes Mars, for instance, Mars first appears to slow down, then come to a stop, then move backward a bit before looping back onto its direct path.

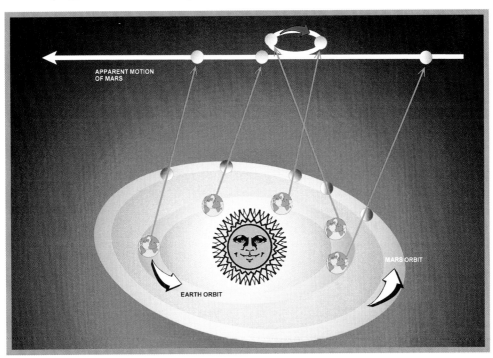

APPARENT MOTION OF MARS

MARS ORBIT

EARTH ORBIT

First because of his religious beliefs. The Roman Catholic Church still clung to the beliefs of Aristotle that Earth did not move, that the Sun revolved around Earth, and that the stars were unchangeable. Second, he felt that Earth was too big and heavy to move as rapidly as Copernicus believed it did. And third, Tycho was never able to see nearby stars appear to shift position against the background of more distant stars over a period of several months. Such a shift, as shown on page 30, is the actual proof that Earth circles the Sun. It is called a *parallax* shift. The reason Tycho could not see the shift was that his observing instruments were not good enough. So, if he could not see a parallax shift, there was none.

However, beginning in 1576, and over the next twenty years, Tycho's observations were to play an important role. They were to provide the very evidence needed to support Copernicus's views, and to cast at least some doubt on Aristotle's.

For instance, in the year 1572 a star in the constellation Cassiopeia exploded and flared up as a star astronomers call a *nova*. Tycho watched the nova for two years from different places in Europe.

Tycho Brahe, the famous astronomer who lost his nose in a duel brought on by an argument over a mathematical problem. Tycho was a keen observer of the planets' changing positions among the background stars. He measured the positions of 777 stars and kept nightly watch over the five then known planets whenever they were visible. He also made the finest observing instruments up to his time. They were set up in his observatory, Uraniborg, build for him in 1576 on the island of Hven by King Frederick of Denmark. Tycho lived from 1546 to 1601.

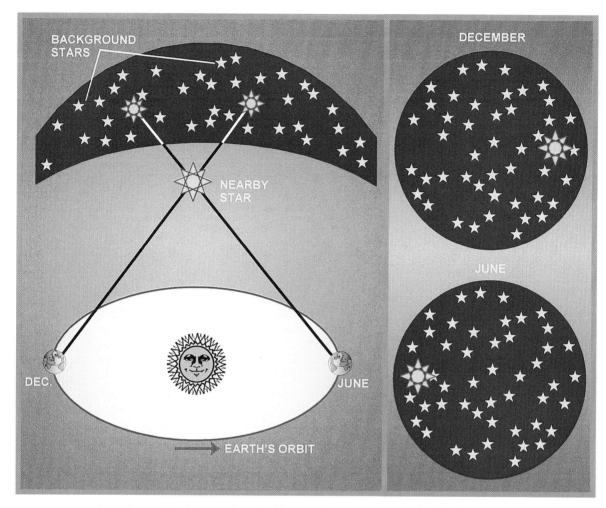

BACKGROUND STARS

NEARBY STAR

DEC.

JUNE

EARTH'S ORBIT

DECEMBER

JUNE

Actual proof that Copernicus had been right in supposing that Earth circled the Sun didn't come until 1840. By that time, observing instruments were good enough to show what astronomers call parallax shift. Here is how it works: A nearby star's position against the background stars is photographed in December. Then six months later, when Earth is half-way around its orbit, the same star's position against the background stars is photographed again. When the two photographs are compared, the nearby star seems to have shifted position. If Earth did not circle the Sun, there would be no parallax shift of the nearby star. Holding your thumb out at arm's length, sighting along it to an object on the other side of the room, and winking one eye then the other will show how parallax works.

He finally concluded that the star was one of the fixed stars, and that the stars can change. So the heavens do change after all. Old Aristotle had been shown to be wrong again.

Tycho's observation of the nova of 1572 made him famous. Over the years he became the most accurate observer of the stars and planets since the times of Hipparchus and Ptolemy, a thousand years earlier. He made his own brass observing instruments, and they were the finest ever. The stars and planets were sighted along them, similar to aiming at a target through the sights of a rifle. The telescope had not yet been invented.

Kepler Solves the Problem

Although Tycho recorded hundreds of observations of Mars and Venus from 1576 to 1591, he didn't have the mathematical skills to make sense out of them. That task was left to a young assistant Tycho hired in 1600. He was twenty-eight-year-old Johannes Kepler, an Austrian high school mathematics teacher. Kepler, it turned out, knew exactly how to make sense out of Tycho's mountains of planetary position plots. Over six years he worked out how the planets move in their *orbits* as they circle the Sun. He

Johann Kepler was the brilliant young assistant to Tycho. By using Tycho's accurate observations of how the planets change position among the background stars, Kepler was able to show just how the planets move in their orbits.

31

was then able to write his famous laws of planetary motion. The laws took a place among the most important discoveries in the history of astronomy. Kepler's first law described the shape of a planet's orbit about the Sun. His second law described how a planet moved along its orbit.

However, one thing kept bothering Kepler. Although he could explain how a planet moves in its orbit, he could not explain what makes it move, and what keeps it moving. He imagined some "mysterious force" from the Sun that held the planets captive and at the same time drove them along. But what that force was he could not say. Even so, the fact that he imagined that such a force existed was a major advance in science.

An Infinite Universe

Before moving on to other giants of astronomy, two other people who lived during Kepler's time should be mentioned. They are important for their far-reaching views about the Solar System's place among the stars. One was the English astronomer Thomas Digges. He envisioned a much larger Universe than the one imagined by Copernicus. Digges thought along these lines: 1) It was Earth's rotation on its axis that made the stars only seem to parade across the sky. 2) Since they didn't actually move that way, there was no reason to suppose that the stars were fixed to a great wheeling glass sphere. 3) Free of that sphere, the stars could lie at many different distances from Earth—some near and others far away, at distances greater than we could even imagine. Detached from that false sphere, the stars also were free to move this way and that. People could not see them move simply because they were so very far away. So the glass spheres of Eudoxus, preserved and polished by Ptolemy, and still believed in by Copernicus, came crashing down. Digges was among the first to say that we live in a Universe that is infinitely large.

The other person we should mention was the Dominican monk Giordano Bruno, who was born in 1548 near Naples, Italy. He was very outspoken and recklessly criticized many church teachings. He was to pay heavily for that recklessness. Among the ideas left in the writings of this remarkable man are these:

In space there are countless constellations, suns, and planets. We see only the suns because they give light. The planets remain invisible, for they are small and dark. There are also

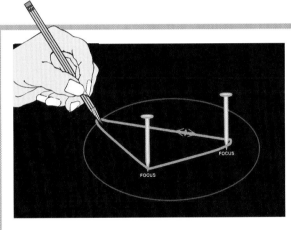

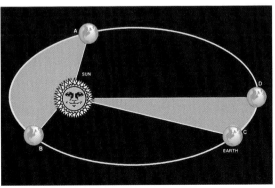

Kepler's first law of planetary motion said that planets move in ellipses (not circles) around the Sun, with the Sun at one focus. Try drawing several ellipses, as shown. But each time, move the two foci (tacks) a bit farther apart to see how the shape of the ellipse changes.

Kepler's second law said that a line from the Sun to a planet sweeps out equal areas in equal time. The two lavender areas—the one swept out from **A** to **B**, and the one swept out from **C** to **D**—have the same areas. When closer to the Sun, the planet moves faster from **A** to **B** than it does when it is farther away (moving from **C** to **D**). The reason is that the Sun's gravitational tug is stronger when the planet is near and so pulls the planet along faster. When the planet is farther away, the Sun's gravitational tug is weaker, and so the planet is pulled along more slowly.

numberless Earths circling around their suns, no worse and no less inhabited than this globe of ours. For no reasonable mind can assume that heavenly bodies which may be far more magnificent than ours would not bear upon them creatures similar or even superior to those upon our human Earth.

Bruno also guessed that the Sun spun around on its axis, that some stars formed pairs, called *binary stars*, and that the Sun did not lie at the center of the Universe. Like Digges, he said that we live in a Universe that has no limits in size. If the Universe had an edge, he asked, then what lay beyond that edge? If the answer is nothing, then the world could be anywhere and, therefore, the Universe could not have a center. With that argument, Bruno removed Earth from the center of creation, which posed a problem that baffles astronomers to this day.

Although Bruno had no proof to back up his ideas, he turned out to be right about most of them, including the Sun's spinning around and double stars. Because he was so outspoken in his criticism of the church, Bruno was arrested, put on trial, found guilty, and then burned alive at the stake in the year 1600.

Four

On the Shoulders of Giants

Galileo Builds a Telescope

About the time Kepler was working out his ideas about how the planets move, another giant of astronomy was gaining a new view of the Universe. He was the Italian scientist Galileo Galilei, born in 1564. Galileo was a university teacher who enjoyed punching holes in widely held scientific beliefs that had not been tested by experiment. This did not make him popular among his fellow professors, because it showed that some of the old and respected masters had been wrong.

Aristotle had taught that the heavier an object was, the faster it fell to the ground. Galileo delighted his students by dropping objects of different weights, at the same time, from a high tower. All the objects struck the ground at the same time. Galileo's insistence that ideas be tested through experiment to find out if they were sound or false earned him the title of "the father of experimental science."

Galileo is best known for being the first to study the heavens through a telescope. In 1609 he turned his homemade instrument on the Moon, planets, and stars. The next year his famous book *The Starry Messenger* told the world of the wonders a telescope reveals. Aristotle had taught that the heavenly bodies were spheres of perfection, smooth and unblemished. Galileo shattered this false notion by describing craters, mountains, valleys,

The Italian astronomer Galileo Galilei was the first to use a telescope to study the heavens. He spotted the four large moons of Jupiter and described to unbelieving listeners mountains, craters, and valleys on the Moon. In this painting done by the Florentine artist L. Sabatelli, Galileo is demonstrating his new telescope to the high official of Venice. Galileo lived from 1564 to 1642.

and other "blemishes" on the Moon. He also discovered dark blemishes in the Sun's surface gases. They came to be called *sunspots*. As he watched the spots move across the solar surface, he correctly concluded that the Sun turns on its axis once every twenty-seven days. His telescope also showed that the hazy band the old Greeks had named the Milky Way was made up of countless stars. He found that Jupiter had four large moons circling it, and he observed that Venus went through phases. That proved that Venus circled the Sun, not Earth.

Galileo's observations made him a firm believer in Copernicus's Solar System, with the Sun at the center. He had no doubts that the church was wrong in its belief of the old Earth-centered system of Aristotle and Ptolemy. Because he was so outspoken, boastful, and smug about his ideas, the church authorities put Galileo on trial for his beliefs and then kept him under house arrest for the rest of his life. They also forbade him to say or write that Earth moved and was not the center of all creation. It was largely Galileo's disrespect and rudeness that brought on his troubles.

Like Kepler, Galileo did not know what force kept the planets in orbit around the Sun. He guessed that all objects in the Universe had some built-in force of attraction for each other, but that's as far as his thinking went. Although he had a vague notion of gravity being the mysterious force, he was not a good enough mathematician to work out the law of gravitation. That was left to the English physicist Isaac Newton.

Newton Writes a Scientific Law

The year Galileo died, 1642, Isaac Newton was born. When he was a student at Cambridge University in 1665, a deadly plague broke out and the students were sent home for a long vacation.

During that time, Newton's interest in mathematics and the motions of the planets set his mind to work. The problem he wanted to solve was what force held the Moon in orbit around Earth and the planets in orbit around the Sun. Why, he wondered, didn't the Moon just go flying off into space? That might have been the most important question that Newton ever asked. It provided the important breakthrough in his thinking about gravitation. And was the force that held the Moon a prisoner of Earth the same force that pulls a stone to the ground when tossed into the air?

Over the next twenty years Newton worked on the problem

Sir Isaac Newton, one of the greatest scientists of all time, worked out the universal law of gravitation. Gravity is the "glue" of the Universe. It holds planets in orbit around their local star, it holds stars together in their galaxies, and it holds you to Earth's surface so that the planet's spinning around doesn't fling you off into space. Newton was an English physicist and mathematician. He lived from 1642 to 1727.

of the motion of objects in space, all the while thinking about gravitation. How did gravitation work? Could he explain it through mathematics? When he tried, he found that he had to invent a new kind of mathematics, which came to be called calculus. When he finally completed his task, he had written a law in physics that became one of the most important of all scientific discoveries. It perfectly explained the force that held the Solar System together. It was gravitation, the force that neither Kepler nor Galileo could understand.

The law also provided a way to figure out how much matter is packed into a star or a planet. The law said that *every object* in the Universe attracts *every* other object, no matter how small or how far away two objects were. The more *mass*, or matter, the objects have, the stronger their force of attraction, and the closer the objects are together, the stronger their gravitational tug on each other. It is Newton's genius that enables scientists today to put artificial satellites in orbit around Earth, and to send space probes to distant parts of the Solar System.

Newton's work didn't end with gravitation. He designed a new kind of telescope. His work with prisms showed that white sunlight contains a rainbow of colors. Not only did he separate white light into all of its colors, but he was able to recombine those colors back into white light again.

Newton died in 1727. By that time people had come to accept Copernicus's Sun-centered Solar System. They also had come to accept Digges's idea of a Universe without end that had more stars than anyone could imagine. The next big problem to be taken on by astronomers was to discover the place of our own star, the Sun, among all those other stars.

Five

Earth's Place in Our Milky Way Home

Halley: "The Stars Move."

Around 1600 Digges had supposed that the stars move past one another. It was left to the English astronomer Edmond Halley to show that they do.

By the time he was sixteen, in 1672, Halley had made up his mind to become an astronomer. He was a very careful observer, and the first serious task the young astronomer set for himself was to prepare a star chart of the southern sky. From the island

The English astronomer Edmond Halley is best known for the comet named after him. This German engraving shows the comet's visit in the year 1682, when Halley first observed it. Using Newton's law of gravitation, Halley plotted the comet's orbit and said it had to be the same comet that was observed centuries earlier, as early as 239 B.C., and again about every seventy years. Halley predicted the comet's return in 1759. He lived from 1656 to 1742.

of Saint Helena, in the South Atlantic, he plotted the positions of 360 stars. Publication of his star catalog started Halley on his rise to fame.

In 1718 Halley compared his own star positions to those plotted by the Greek astronomers Hipparchus and Ptolemy more than a thousand years earlier. He was surprised to find that the three bright stars Arcturus, Betelgeuse, and Sirius had slightly changed their positions over the centuries. Here was convincing evidence that the stars move. That meant that the ageless constellations were ever so slowly changing their shapes.

Why can't we see a star change its position among the other stars? The answer is because the stars are so very far away. You could watch a star every night for your entire life and not find that it has moved, even though the star actually is speeding along at thousands of miles an hour. The farther away the star is, the slower its motion appears across the sky. Imagine two jet airliners flying along at exactly the same speed. One is only 5,000 feet (1,525 meters) above the ground, while the other is at a height of 50,000 feet (15,238 meters). The low flying jet

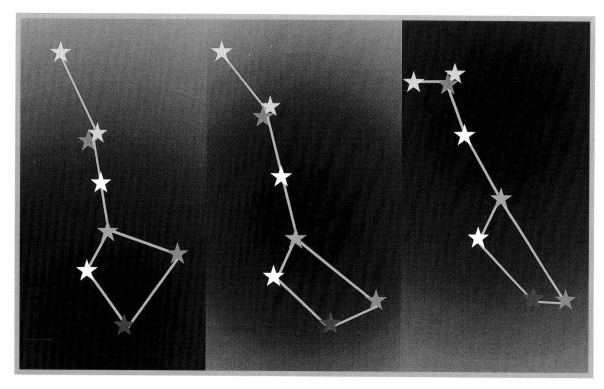

Although the constellations seem eternal, they are not. As Halley correctly pointed out, the stars move in relation to each other, so a constellation's shape is always changing. A hundred thousand years ago, the shape of the Big Dipper (which is an asterism, not a constellation) was different from its shape today. And a hundred thousand years from now it will be still different.

NORTH

EAST

WES

SOUTH

Careful study of the motions of the stars give a bewildering picture. They seem to be moving every which way and at different speeds, indicated by the length of the arrows. Astronomers of the 1700s wondered if the universe of stars was a chaos of motion, or if eventually patterns of order would be revealed.

EARTH'S

PLACE

IN

OUR

MILKY

WAY

HOME

tears across your field of view in only a second or so, while the higher flying one seems to creep along at a snail's pace. That same distance effect also works for the stars. A far away star appears to move much more slowly than a nearby star, even though they are both moving at the same speed across our view.

After Halley's discovery that the stars move, astronomers

EARTH'S

PLACE

IN

OUR

MILKY

WAY

HOME

began to ask if our own star, the Sun, also moved through space. Or was it fixed and motionless at the center of the Universe of stars?

Herschel: "The Sun Moves."

Draw a circle about the size of your fist in the sky and count the stars inside the circle. If you worked out the way each of those stars is moving, you would find a helter-skelter pattern with the stars moving every which way, as shown on page 43. Do the stars actually move that way, or is there an orderly pattern to their movement?

That was a question William Herschel wondered about in the late 1700s. Herschel was born in Germany in 1738 but moved to England, where he became a music teacher and an amateur astronomer. He made the best telescopes the world had known. On the night of March 13, 1781, he spotted a fuzzy object in the constellation Gemini the Twins. Night after night he watched the object creep slowly eastward among the stars. It turned out to be the planet Uranus. Herschel became famous overnight for becoming the first person in recorded history to discover a new planet. The discovery doubled the size of the Solar System, for Uranus was twice Saturn's distance from the Sun.

Two years later he made an even more important discovery. As Halley had announced that the stars move, Herschel was able to announce, "The Sun is in motion through space."

The English music teacher who became an amateur astronomer, Sir William Herschel, was the first person in history to discover an unknown planet. The planet was Uranus, and he discovered it in 1781. Herschel made the finest telescopes of his time. The one shown here was an 18-inch (45-centimeter) reflecting telescope built in 1800.

By Herschel's time, fine telescopes had enabled astronomers to tell in what direction and at what speed a star was moving relative to the Sun. Herschel drew direction arrows for about a dozen stars. Some of the arrows flared out from a point in the constellation Hercules. Others seemed to close in toward a distant point in the opposite part of the sky, in the constellation Columba. He understood that the flaring out in one direction and closing in in the opposite direction were optical illusions caused by the Sun's actual motion toward Hercules. Today we know that the Sun is speeding toward the constellation Cygnus the Swan at 137 miles (220 kilometers) a second.

You experience the same optical illusion while driving along a superhighway. The trees and other landscape features ahead appear to be rushing toward you and flaring out. But when you view them through the rear window, they stream away from you toward a distant point on the horizon.

In 1803 Herschel discovered that Bruno had been right about the existence of binary, or double, stars. He found that the bright star Castor in the constellation Gemini the Twins had a faint companion revolving about it. Here was proof that Newton's law of gravitation worked out among the stars just as it works within the Solar System.

A Shape for the Galaxy

Herschel, his sister Caroline, and his son John also tackled the problem of trying to discover the shape of that vast city of stars we call the Milky Way Galaxy. Herschel wanted to find Earth's position within the Galaxy. His 18-inch (46-centimeter) telescope revealed about ten million stars. He started by pointing his telescope in various directions and counting the number of stars in circular patches all around the sky. When a patch contained a lot of stars, Herschel reasoned that the stars stretched off to a great distance. When a patch contained only a few stars, he reasoned that they stretched away to a shorter distance.

Herschel's son John carried on the work in the Southern Hemisphere. In all, the two made about six-thousand star counts over several years. By comparing them and arranging them like pieces of a jigsaw puzzle, Herschel concluded that our galaxy was shaped like a giant powder puff and that the Sun was just about in the middle.

That view of the Milky Way remained pretty much unchanged until the early 1900s. The man to change the view was the American astronomer Harlow Shapley. Around 1918 he reasoned that we look in toward the center of the Milky Way Galaxy in the direction of the constellation Sagittarius. Why? Because the sky in that direction is most crowded with stars. Off in the opposite direction, in the constellation Auriga, the sky is least crowded with stars. He said that we are looking out of the Galaxy in that direction. But Shapley's telescope had given him another clue about where the center of the Galaxy lies.

He had seen many ball-shaped collections of stars called *globular clusters*. A typical globular cluster has 100,000 or more stars. Almost all of the globular clusters Shapley could see were also off in the direction of Sagittarius. Only a few were in the opposite direction of Auriga, where the sky was less crowded. Could it be, he wondered, that the globular clusters were arranged around the center of the Galaxy? If so, then the center of the Galaxy would be the same as the center of the grouping of globular clusters. It turned out that he was right. When he then measured the distance to stars in the globular clusters, he found that the Sun was not near the center of the Galaxy at all but way out near the edge.

EARTH'S
PLACE
IN
OUR
MILKY
WAY
HOME

Globular clusters of stars gave Harlow Shapley a way of locating the Sun's position in the Milky Way. He found that we are not located in the center of the galaxy but way out near the edge. The globular cluster seen here is one of the brightest known. It is a mammoth ball of some 300-thousand old and aging stars known as G1 that orbits the Andromeda Galaxy.

Shapley estimated the distance to the center of the Galaxy, but he came up with a number more than twice as big as the actual distance. The reason for his error was that he was peering through clouds of gas and dust that block our view of the central regions of our galactic home. The dust makes those faraway stars appear dimmer than they are, and so they seem farther away than they actually are. And so Shapley was misled.

EARTH'S
PLACE
IN
OUR
MILKY
WAY
HOME

If we were able to see our home galaxy from a great distance, it would look much like this view of the open spiral galaxy NGC891. Because we are looking at the galaxy edge-on, we cannot see the spiral arms. Like the Milky Way, NGC891 has a dense band of dust that blocks our view of many of the galaxy's stars. Another spiral galaxy, M51, viewed not edge-on, but from above, clearly displays spiral arms winding out from the dense nucleus of stars at the center. The gravitational tug of a smaller companion galaxy pulls one of the spiral arms out of shape.

To appreciate the sizes and distances involved in astronomy, you must become familiar with a unit of measure called a *light-year*. It is the distance that light travels in one year at the speed of about 186,000 miles a second (300,000 kilometers a second). That amounts to some 6 trillion miles (some 10 trillion kilometers) a year. So one light-year equals 6 trillion miles.

The Milky Way: Our Galactic Home

Enclosing the central region of our galaxy is a loosely knit cocoon of globular clusters that forms a spherical halo about 130,000 light-years in diameter. At the very center is the *galactic nucleus*, about 33,000 light-years across. Stretching outward from the nucleus is the *galactic disk*. The disk contains most of the Galaxy's matter—stars, gas, and dust. It is arranged in about five graceful spiral arms that form, dissolve, and re-form over millions of years. Because of the large open spaces between the spiral arms, we call our galaxy an *open spiral galaxy*. We see many others like it, such as M51.

The whole system of spiral arms, stars, gas, and dust spins around. That means that the stars circle the central hub in much the same way that the planets circle the Sun. Traveling at 137 miles (220 kilometers) a second, it takes the Sun 225 million years to make one trip around the Galaxy. That time is called a *cosmic year*.

The Galaxy contains young and hot blue stars, cooler yellow

EARTH'S
PLACE
IN
OUR
MILKY
WAY
HOME

stars like the Sun, and giant stars in their old age that shine with a red light. There also are smaller red stars that seem ageless because they have the longest life spans of all. The older reddish stars are mostly in the globular clusters and in the galactic nucleus. The younger bluish stars are found mostly in the spiral arms. It is here in the spiral arms that we find those vast clouds of gas and dust, called *nebulae*. The nebulae are the birth places of stars, for stars form out of these dense clouds of matter. How many stars make up the Galaxy? Although an accurate count is impossible, our best guesses range from 300 billion to 500 billion stars. How old is the Galaxy? Today our best guess is about 15 billion years old.

The Milky Way, our galaxy home, is a vast city of stars surrounded by a halo of globular clusters of old stars. The nucleus of the galaxy is hidden from our view by clouds of cosmic dust. From edge to opposite edge, the Milky Way is some 100,000 light-years. The Sun is located in the galactic disk some 30,000 light-years from the nucleus.

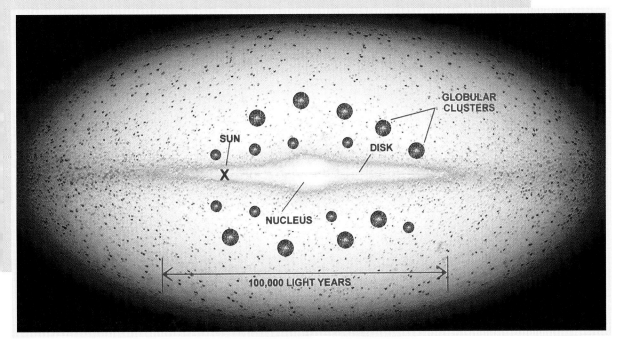

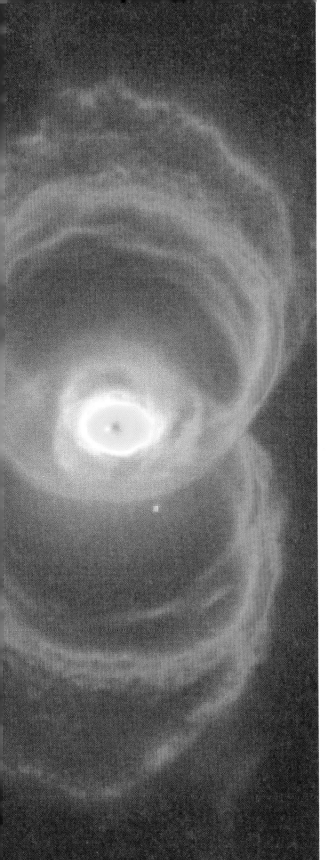

Astronomers can think of no place else in the Universe, except in the nebulae, to look for the cradles of star creation. The Hubble Space Telescope has given us some remarkably beautiful images of many different kinds of nebulae.

On the far left, bottom, are gaseous pillars known as the Eagle Nebula in the nebula known as M16. The columns, looking like enchanted space castles, are made of hydrogen gas and dust rising out of a dark cloud base. Located some 7,000 light-years away in the constellation Serpens, the tip of each column is large enough to contain the entire Solar System. The especially dark globules of gas and dust are new stars in the making.

At left is is the planetary nebula MyCn18, the Hourglass Nebula. It is gaseous debris cast-off into space by a dying Sun-like star. Most Sun-like stars probably go through a planetary nebula stage before ending their lives as red giants and then white dwarfs. Planetary nebulae have nothing to do with planets. They were given their name long ago by astronomers who confused the gaseous blobs with planets. The small white dot just off center within the blue region is the dying star causing the hourglass to glow.

At top far left another planetary nebula, the Cat's Eye Nebula, or NGC6543. It is a very complex nebula with knots of gas, jets of high-speed gas, and shells within shells. It seems to be fairly young, only a thousand years old. The bright star in the center is the dying star that expelled the gaseous halo.

The remaining image is a Hubble Heritage Team photo of the dwarf galaxy NGC7742, which might have been nicknamed the Fried Egg. It seems to be a very active galaxy with star formation taking place in the lumpy thin ring around the core, or yolk of the egg.

Six

Our Galaxy's Place in Space

Beyond the Milky Way

For centuries astronomers thought of the vast collection of stars seen in the Milky Way as the entire Universe. Possibly the stars just stretched away endlessly, becoming dimmer and dimmer with distance until they faded from view. Or maybe there was a limit. Maybe the Milky Way was a neat arrangement of stars, and beyond its edge there was nothing but a dark, empty sea of outer space that stretched away forever.

In 1750 the English astronomer Thomas Wright was among the first to puzzle over certain small fuzzy patches among the stars. The French astronomer Charles Messier found the objects bothersome because he kept mistaking them for comets, which

In 1924, the American astronomer Edwin Hubble was the first to show that the other "island universes," or galaxies, fill space far beyond the Milky Way. He further showed that all the galaxies appear to be rushing away from us in a Universe that is expanding. The more distant a galaxy, the faster it rushing away. Hubble lived from 1889 to 1953.

were his main interest. But being a good observer, Messier faithfully recorded the positions of the fuzzy nebulae. In 1784 he published a catalog listing the locations of 103 of the objects. Wright began to wonder if the nebulae might possibly be galaxies similar to our own but at very great distances outside our system of stars. He became convinced that the Milky Way had boundaries, an island universe floating in space. Herschel, too, wondered if the fuzzy patches were other worlds. He asked, "Does this mean there is more than 'one universe'?"

The Universe Grows Larger

It wasn't for 120 years, in 1924, that those questions were answered. The man to answer them was the American astronomer Edwin Hubble, after whom the Hubble Space Telescope was named. He took special interest in the nebula in the constellation Andromeda the Chained Woman. It is known as M 31, the 31st "bothersome" object in Messier's catalog, or simply the Andromeda Galaxy.

As Hubble studied the fuzzy patch through the 100-inch (2.5-meter) telescope at California's Mount Wilson Observatory, he could pick out individual stars. On observing those stars night after night, he noticed that some of them changed from bright to dim and back to bright again. They were a class of stars called *variable stars*, which go through cycles, or *periods*, of brightening

Using the Hale telescope, Edwin Hubble studied a special class of variable stars visible in the Andromeda Galaxy, known as M31, to make the first distance estimate to a galaxy beyond our own. The galaxy turned out to be more than two million light-years away. Find the great square of the constellation Pegasus, then, using binoculars, locate the tiny fuzzy patch of M31 in Andromeda.

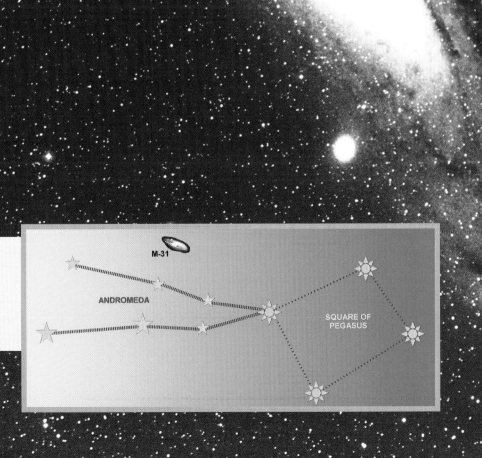

M-31

ANDROMEDA

SQUARE OF
PEGASUS

and dimming. Some complete a period in only an hour or so. Others have longer periods measured in weeks or months.

In the early 1900s, astronomers discovered something very useful about the class of variable stars Hubble was timing. They are called *Cepheid variables*, named after the first such star identified in the constellation Cepheus the King. The longer the period of a Cepheid, the brighter the star is. This important relationship between a Cepheid's period and its brightness was discovered by Henrietta S. Leavitt in 1912. There are many Cepheids in the Milky Way, so astronomers are quite familiar with them. Since Hubble was able to time the period of Andromeda's Cepheids, he knew their actual brightness. Knowing that brightness enabled him to estimate their distance. All he had to do was measure how bright they appeared to be from their great distance and then use a special law of light to estimate that distance. The Andromeda Galaxy, he announced, was one million light-years away. But could that one distance measurement be reliable? Was there a way to check it?

Nova stars helped provide more evidence. When nova stars in the Milky Way flare up and reach their brightest, they are about a hundred thousand times brighter than the Sun. Several nova stars were visible in M 31. Probably they behaved much the same as the Milky Way's nova stars. If so, then they also could be used as cosmic yardsticks. When astronomers measured how bright the nova stars appeared to be after their light crossed space and reached their telescopes, that special law of light could be used, as before, to reveal distance. Nova measurements gave a distance of not one, but two million light-years. Which figure was right?

Brightness measurements of globular clusters in Andromeda also gave a distance of about 2 million light-years, as did brightness measurements of certain very massive and super bright stars called *supergiants*. Those are the bluish white stars seen at the edges of our galaxy's spiral arms. The Andromeda Galaxy turned out to be a spiral galaxy very much like our own. It is the only giant spiral galaxy close enough to study in detail. Its distance is now known to be 2.3 million light-years, more than twenty times the distance across the Milky Way. What misled Hubble originally was that there were two types of Cepheids—one brighter than the other. Hubble did not realize that the Andromeda Galaxy contained the brighter class of Cepheids, and that is what made him think that Andromeda was closer than it actually is.

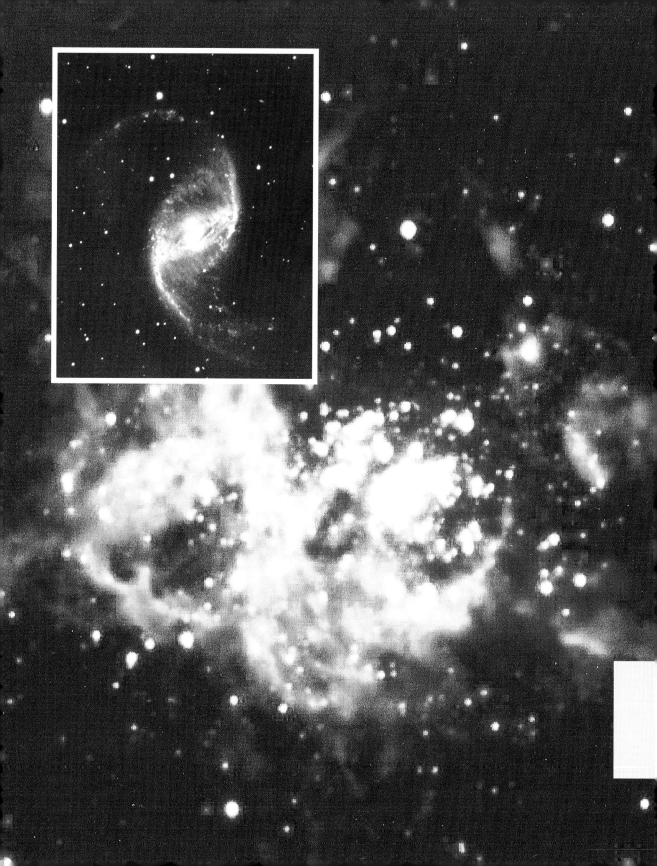

Seven

Galaxies Galore

With the discovery of the Andromeda Galaxy's great distance, the size of the Universe took another giant leap. Earth became a humble rock held gravitationally captive by an average type star amid billions of other stars. And we were no longer alone in space. The Universe continued to grow with the discovery that more and more of Messier's "bothersome" objects were galaxies, not just patches of foggy dust and gas.

The number of "island universes" in the heavens staggers the imagination. A good telescope brings into view more galaxies than the number of stars seen by the unaided eye. If you examined only the bowl of the Big Dipper, you would find at least half a million galaxies there! The Hubble Space Telescope

There are more galaxies than we can count, and they come in a wide variety of forms. At left is the Large Magellanic Cloud, a shapeless captive galaxy of the Milky Way and closest galaxy to us. The green gaseous filaments form the Tarantula Nebula (NGC2070), a region of active star formation. Inset is the beautiful barred spiral galaxy NGC1530 seen in the constellation Camelopardalis.

can see billions of galaxies. How many more lie out there in the dark beyond our sight is anyone's guess.

Clusters of Galaxies

Galaxies seem to come in groups rather than existing as lone stellar islands. In our region of space is a cluster of about two dozen galaxies. We call it the Local Group. Among them are two other spiral galaxies and two irregular galaxies that are small satellite galaxies of the Milky Way. They are called the Large

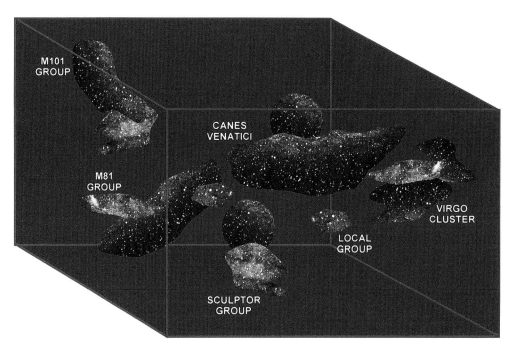

The Local Supercluster is a cluster of galaxy clusters. Our galaxy, the Milky Way, is one of some two dozen making up the Local Group galaxy cluster. In all, more than a dozen galaxy clusters stretching across almost 100 million light-years make up the Local Supercluster. Gravitation is the cosmic "glue" that holds these large-scale structures together. The very idea of such collections of galaxies would have astounded astronomers such as Ptolemy, Galileo, and Tycho.

Each fuzzy patch and each dot in this Hubble image is a galaxy, but the seemingly endless number of them covers only a tiny speck of the sky. To produce this deep-sky image of the Universe, Hubble viewed the patch of sky in the constellation Ursa Major for ten days. The nearest galaxies seen here are about 2.5 billion light-years away; the most distant are about 10.5 billion light-years away. Their sizes range from 3,000 to 55,000 light-years in diameter.

Magellanic Cloud and the Small Magellanic Cloud, named after the Portuguese navigator Ferdinand Magellan. The Andromeda Galaxy, a member of the Local Group, also has satellite companion galaxies. At one end of the galaxy size scale in the Local Group are the giant spirals like us and Andromeda. At the other end are a half dozen or so dwarf galaxies. Of all the galaxies we can see in the Universe, most are dwarfs. But the sheer size and brightness of the giant spiral galaxies—and large sphere-shaped galaxies called *ellipticals*—make those galaxy types the most noticeable, so they dominate the sky.

Lots of galaxies in a cluster means lots of mass, and lots of mass means strong gravitational attraction among the galaxies in a cluster. All that force of attraction pulls the galaxies into a ball-shaped cloud, with the larger galaxies near the center. Smaller clusters with only a dozen or so galaxies tend to be more spread out. The weaker gravitational attraction among those small galaxies allows a looser grouping. Our Local Group is one such loose collection of galaxies.

Superclusters and the Great Wall

Clusters of galaxies stretch away into space in all directions. Many of them group as *superclusters*. Astronomers can estimate the distance to and size of superclusters by studying particular galaxies within a supercluster. It works the same way as Hubble's use of Cepheid variable stars to measure the distance to the Andromeda Galaxy. But instead of measuring the light from individual stars, the astronomer measures the light from an entire galaxy within the supercluster. This supercosmic yardstick has given us cluster distances of billions of light-years.

A supercluster in the constellation Virgo has more than a thousand galaxies and is more than 52 million light-years away. One in the constellation Hercules is more than 470 million light-years away. One of the most distant of all superclusters is one in the constellation Hydra. It is some 2.5 billion light-years away.

In recent years the astronomers John Huchra and Margaret Geller have even discovered clusters of superclusters. One lies some 330 million light-years away from us. Because it is some

30 times broader than it is thick, this enormous collection of galaxies has been named the *Great Wall*. A grouping of so many galaxies makes the Great Wall a gravity monster able to tug on very distant galaxy clusters and so influence their motion. But there is an *even more massive gravity monster only 130 million light-years away called the *Great Attractor*. It was discovered by four astronomers—Alan Dressler, Sandra Faber, David Burstein, and Gary Wegner. Although our telescopes have yet to spot the Great Attractor, we can feel its gravitational tug. By measuring the strength of that tug, we think the Great Attractor may be made up of ten thousand or more galaxies the size of the Milky Way. Its strong gravitation seems to be pulling surrounding clusters and superclusters in toward its center.

As bigger and better telescopes, such as Hubble, are built, more such monstrous galactic pieces of the Universe are being discovered. Because we have so much more to learn about them, they are the new frontier in the study of the Universe.

Eight

Galaxies on the Move

An Expanding Universe

By 1930, Hubble and other astronomers had studied enough galaxies to be sure of one thing. Except for a few nearby galaxies, the thousands upon thousands of other galaxies were all rushing away from us. Only the Andromeda Galaxy and a few others in the Local Group were approaching. The speed of the rushing-away galaxies seemed hard to believe. Many were flying off at rates up to 10,000 miles a second (16,000 kilometers a second).

Hubble then discovered something else. The more distant a group of galaxies from us, the faster the group was speeding away. Look at the list of galaxies and clusters of galaxies on the next page. They are arranged in order of distance from us. As the distance becomes greater, notice what happens to the speed of

The Hubble Space Telescope as seen in the cargo bay of the space shuttle Endeavour. *This photograph was taken during the servicing mission that replaced the two solar array panels. The panels provide energy that drives the telescope. At the time of the photograph a large area of Earth was covered by cloud.*

the galaxy or cluster. No matter in what part of the sky we point the great telescopes, the picture is the same. Galaxies and clusters of galaxies are flying away from us at tremendous speeds.

Galaxy	Speed (Kilometers per sec)	Distance (Millions of light-years)
M 64	150	7
M 82	300	13
M 63	450	18
M 65	805	25
M 96	950	29
M 60	1,100	38

Cluster	Speed	Distance
Coma	6,700	291
Pegasus II	12,714	490
Leo	19,500	847
Ursa Major 2	40,233	1,560
Hydra	60,600	2,600
3C 295	137,758	5,700

To picture what is happening to all those galaxies, imagine a half-inflated balloon with small galaxy dots stuck onto it. Each dot represents a galaxy. As the balloon is inflated and expands, the distance between the dots gets larger all around the balloon's surface.

Now imagine that you are on one of those galaxy-dots, any one. As the balloon swells, every other galaxy-dot around you would appear to be moving away from you. From your position, you would seem to be at the center of things, at the center of an expanding universe of galaxies. And if you moved to another galaxy, you would see exactly the same thing. No matter which galaxy you chose, the view would be the same. Every galaxy would appear to be at the center of a universe of galaxies expanding away from you at breakneck speed.

What Are Quasars?

When we look at a galaxy that is fifty million light-years away, we are seeing that galaxy as it was fifty million years ago, not as it is at the present moment. The light reaching us from that galaxy has taken fifty million years to cross that immense distance of fifty million light-years. When we look at the Hydra cluster, for example, we are seeing those galaxies as they were 2.6 billion years ago. So telescopes are time machines that can take us back billions of years into the past of the Universe.

Among the most distant—and oldest—objects we can see are *quasars*. They shine with a bluish light and are extremely bright and energetic. They also are very puzzling. A quasar

The Universe of galaxies is expanding. Astronomers of old could not even have imagined that such a thing was happening. But today's telescopes show that all the galaxies are rushing away from each other. The more distant a galaxy, the faster it is moving away from us and all other galaxies. To picture what is happening, imagine a flat balloon with pennies stuck onto it. As the balloon is blown-up more and more, the pennies stuck to its surface move farther and farther away from each other (top). The same is true of the galaxies. As space expands more and more, all of the galaxies and clusters of galaxies move farther and farther away from each other (bottom).

releases enough energy in one second to supply all of Earth's electrical needs for a billion years. Astronomers now think that these stellar powerhouses are ancient galaxies, but we see them at the time they were forming, when the Universe was young. One quasar is more than ten thousand times brighter than the Milky Way. Some are so distant that they travel at close to the speed of light. Some lie at distances of several billion light-years. The most distant quasars we can see seem to be about 12 billion light-years away. That means that we may be looking back 12 billion years in time and seeing a galaxy being formed. Right now we simply do not know if that is the case. In 1997 astronomers spotted the most distant object ever observed. It was a galaxy 12.2 billion light-years away. The puzzle of the origin of the galaxies, and of the Universe, is astronomy's superproblem. Although astronomers have been making progress in the past few years, the solution is not yet in sight.

The fact that we see quasars mostly at great distances—that is, mostly during the early life of the Universe—makes most astronomers think that the Universe changes with time. Other astronomers think that the Universe has always been pretty much as it is today.

Where Is the Universe Going?

If change has been the rule in the Universe, then how may it change in the future? The fact that we see practically all of the galaxies rushing away from us, and from each other, today poses some interesting questions about the future. For one, will the Universe just keep on expanding forever?

Newton showed that it is gravity that holds the Universe, including the Solar System, together. His law of gravitation also explains why large clusters of galaxies are held together in a ball shape with most of the large galaxies collected near the center. Smaller clusters with only a dozen or so galaxies tend to be more spread out. The weaker gravitational attraction allows for a looser grouping. Such a gravity "glue" also applies to the Universe at large.

The key word is mass, or matter. If there is enough matter in the Universe, gravitational attraction would apply a braking action to the expansion and slow it down. The galaxies would then one day stop in their tracks, pause for a cosmic moment, and then slowly begin to tumble inward toward one another. Instead of expanding, the cosmic balloon would shrink. This would end in a gigantic collision of all matter in the Universe. Many astronomers think that the collision would produce an explosion of all that matter. The matter would then form new galaxies in a born-again Universe that would start expanding all over again. If that is the case, then the Universe might just keep on expanding and collapsing and expanding again forever. Maybe the Universe never had a beginning and will never end. Maybe there are only endless cycles of change.

Now we must ask what would happen if there is *not* enough matter in the Universe to put on the gravitational brakes and stop the expansion? We would then be living in a Universe that would just keep on expanding forever. As it did, perhaps its galaxies would age and die as their stars burned out until the galaxies became dark, dead places. Or perhaps certain other galaxies would collide and become enriched with new energy and matter. New stars and planets aplenty would form. Then, for several billion years more, such galaxies might thrive for a cosmic while before they burned out also. In the very long run, the Universe would become cold and dark.

In 1998 astronomers proposed an idea that would have

baffled Newton. There may be a force called "cosmological repulsion." In short, anti-gravity. Instead of causing galaxies to attract one another, anti-gravity would be pushing them apart. This would cause the expansion of the Universe to speed up with time. If this new idea turns out to be true, then a re-collapse of the Universe could never take place.

No one knows the answers to these questions. In a way, we are like the old Greek astronomers. We yearn to know but do not yet have the skills to answer our questions. As our new century begins, we have a large store of questions about the Universe and our place in it. It will be interesting for astronomers of the future to see how many of them have been answered by the time the next century ends.

Apparent brightness—the measure of a celestial object's observed brightness; how bright the object appears to the eye. The farther away a light source is from the observer, the less its apparent brightness will be, although its actual brightness does not change.

Astronomy—the science dealing with celestial bodies, their distances, luminosities, sizes, motions, relative positions, composition, and structure. The word comes from the Greek and means the "arrangement of the stars."

Binary star—two stars held in gravitational association with each other and revolving around a common center of mass. Also called double stars.

Cepheid variables—hot white and yellow giant variable stars with periods ranging from a few hours to about fifty days. They are used as cosmic yardsticks to measure distances to galaxies beyond the Milky Way. Their brightness is related directly to their periods.

Cluster—a group of from a few dozen to hundreds or thousands of galaxies. Our galaxy, the Milky Way, belongs to a small cluster called the Local Group. Also, there are groups, or clusters, of closely associated stars. The Pleiades are one such open cluster.

Constellation—the grouping into imaginary figures of certain stars on the celestial sphere. The ancients recognized the groups as human and animal figures; for example, Orion the Hunter, Leo the Lion, and so on. By international agreement, astronomers recognize a total of eighty-eight constellations.

Cosmic year—about 225 million years, which is the time it takes the Sun to complete one revolution about the nucleus of our galaxy.

Ecliptic—the path the Sun and planets appear to follow around the sky in one year. It forms a great circle on the celestial sphere.

Elliptical galaxy—a galaxy shaped like an enormous sphere rather than a flat, spread-out galaxy such as our spiral galaxy, the Milky Way.

Epicycles—circular loops imagined by ancient astronomers in an attempt to account for the back-and-forth observed motions of the planets. The supposed loops are optical illusions resulting from observing the planets from a planet that itself is moving.

Fixed stars—all the stars visible to us. Since stargazers of ancient times were not able to detect the stars' motions in relation to one another, they called them fixed stars.

Galactic disk—the broad, rather flat region of a spiral galaxy that extends outward from and spins around the central region (nucleus) of the galaxy.

Galactic nucleus—the central region of a galaxy.

Galaxy—a vast collection of stars, gas, and dust held together gravitationally.

Globular cluster—a collection of tens or hundreds of thousands of stars forming a globular shape. A halo of about one hundred globular clusters forms a sphere around the central part of our galaxy.

Gravitation—the force of attraction between any two or more objects in the Universe. The greater the mass, the greater the force of attraction; the greater the distance, the less the force of attraction.

Great attractor—an especially massive collection of galaxies that we cannot see but which we can detect as a result of its gravitational attraction. The strength of its gravitational tug suggests that it may contain ten thousand galaxies the size of the Milky Way.

Great wall—a cluster of superclusters of galaxies some thirty times broader than it is thick. Its shape suggested its name.

Light-year—the distance that light travels in one year, at the rate of 186,000 miles (300,000 kilometers) per second, which is about 6 trillion miles (10 trillion kilometers).

Magnitude—(apparent or visual)—the relative visual brightness of the stars as we see them in the sky. The higher the magnitude number of a star, the fainter the star appears to us. Some of the nearby stars that appear brightest have a magnitude of 1, and are said to be first magnitude stars. Stars that appear 2.5 times dimmer than first magnitude stars have a visual magnitude of 2, and stars appearing 2.5 times dimmer than second magnitude stars have a visual magnitude of 3, and so on. The faintest stars visible to the unaided eye are magnitude 6.

Mass—a given quantity of matter of any kind, or the total amount of matter contained in an object.

Milky Way—the name of our local galaxy, containing some 300 billion to 500 billion or more stars. Also the name of that hazy band of light seen in the summer and winter sky. A small telescope resolves the band into countless stars.

Nebula—a great cloud of dust and gas within a galaxy.

Nova—a star that, for some reason not yet fully understood, bursts into brilliance. Within a few days a typical nova may become hundreds or thousands of times brighter than usual, then it becomes somewhat less brilliant, and after a few months or longer the star returns to its prenova brightness.

Open spiral galaxy—a galaxy, such as the Milky Way, that has spiral arms with relatively empty lanes between them.

Orbit—the path one celestial object traces as it moves around another to which it is attracted by the force of gravitation.

Parallax—the apparent shift in the position of an object when viewed from two different locations.

Period—the time a variable star takes to complete one cycle of going from bright to dim and back again to bright. The periods of some variables are measured in hours, while the periods of others are measured in weeks or months. A period is also the time it takes one object to orbit another.

Planet—a celestial object that shines by reflected light from a star around which the planet is held gravitationally captive.

Precession—a gradual change in the direction of the tilt of Earth's axis due to gravitational attraction by the Sun and the Moon. The combined attractions cause Earth to wobble like a spinning top slowing down. The axis completes one rotation in about 26,000 years.

Quasars—extremely bright and very distant objects that seem to be the hearts of galaxies that were forming when the Universe was young.

Revolution—the motion of one celestial body around another. The Moon revolves about Earth; the planets revolve around the Sun.

Rotation—the spinning of a body around its axis. The Sun and all of the planets rotate. Earth completes one rotation about every twenty-four hours.

Solar System—the Sun, its planets accompanied by about sixty known satellites, plus many lesser objects, including comets, asteroids, and meteoroids.

Star—a large hot, glowing globe of gases that emits energy through a process called nuclear fusion. The Sun is a typical, and our closest, star.

Sunspots—great dark spots about the size of Earth that break out in the Sun's lower atmosphere. They become especially numerous about every eleven years. They are magnetic storms of upwelling gases that cool when they break out of the Sun and so appear darker than surrounding hotter gases.

Supercluster—a cluster of clusters of galaxies.

Supergiants—enormous young stars that are very massive, that shine with a bluish white light, and that have relatively short life spans.

Variable star—a star that is not uniform in brightness, becoming bright, reaching "maximum," then dim, reaching "minimum." The cycle repeats itself over periods of hours, months, or years.

Wandering stars—the planets. They were called "wandering" stars by stargazers of ancient times because they were seen to move eastward among the "fixed" stars across the great sky dome.

Zodiac—the band of constellations, recognized since ancient times, that circles the sky and through which the Sun and planets appear to move.

Andrade, E.N. da C. *Sir Isaac Newton: His Life and Work.* Garden City, NY: Doubleday Anchor Books, 1954.

Cowan, Ron. "Cosmologists in Flatland." *Science News* (February 28, 1998) pp. 139–141.

Galileo. *Discoveries and Opinions of Galileo.* Translated by Stillman Drake. Garden City, NY: Doubleday Anchor Books, 1957.

Gallant, Roy A. *Astrology: Sense or Nonsense?* Garden City, NY: Doubleday, 1974.

_____. *The Constellations: How They Came to Be.* New York: Four Winds, 1979; and New York: Macmillan, 1991.

_____. *Once Around the Galaxy.* New York: Franklin Watts, 1983.

_____. *Our Universe.* Washington, DC: National Geographic, 1994.

Peterson, Ivars. "Circles in the Sky: Detecting the Shape of the Universe." *Science News.* (February 21, 1998) pp. 123–125.

Ronan, Colin A. *The Astronomers.* London: Evans Brothers, 1964.

Santillana, Giorgio de. The Crime of Galileo. Chicago: University of Chicago Press, 1955.

Sullivant, Rosemary. "When the Apple Falls." *Astronomy.* (April 1998) pp. 55–59.

Index